Self Sabotage

Laura A. Felix

BookLeaf
Publishing

India | USA | UK

Presentation by *BookLeaf Publishing*

Web: www.bookleafpub.com

E-mail: info@bookleafpub.com

ISBN: 9789357696371

First edition 2023

DEDICATION

Dedicated to my childhood best friend, Adriana Perez, who left this world too early. She was at the top of our reading program and helped me with grammar throughout college. I'm grateful for her friendship and honored to have had her in my life.

The poem:

"Why am I not what I am?

What I feel is not rancor or lack of love, but tears from the heart with disappointment and loss of illusion.

I was a prisoner of a bitter and painful game, a piece on a table surrounded by fire.

Your false caresses and deceitful words broke the walls surrounding my heart.

Loneliness accompanied me when I ran after the crumbs of your mismatched love.

Feelings that stabbed my heart with thorns touched by the poison of heartbreak.

Because I don't appreciate or claim the stakes that this move left in my heart.

In my soul, there is only hope and faith to fight to recover what I am."

Written by ~Adriana Perez.

May she rest in power.

ACKNOWLEDGEMENT

I want to express my eternal gratitude to Adriana Perez, to whom this book is dedicated. She has been instrumental in helping me express myself through reading and writing since childhood.

My family has been an unwavering source of support during, they have consistently provided comfort, accountability, and encouragement as I strive for happiness in my writing.

I would like to extend a special thanks to Dr. Dawn Michaux James for her coaching, which has empowered me to make life-changing adjustments to achieve a positive mind, body, and soul. Her compassionate, non-judgmental approach has allowed me to thrive and engage in healthy relationships, fulfilling my life's purpose.

Lastly, I am grateful to Kelly France for helping me find creative outlets, increasing my self-confidence, encouraging me to write, and guiding me as I embark on a healing journey through counseling.

PREFACE

In her book, Laura A. Felix shares personal stories to inspire and encourage others to heal from their past experiences. As the eldest child of Mexican migrants, she grew up in an inner-city community surrounded by Mexican Americans before moving to the suburbs. In her writing, she reflects on the challenges she faced in both environments. These stories come from her own timeline of experiences, which she uncovered through meditation, mental health counseling, and life coaching.

Chicana

"an American woman or girl of Mexican descent"
.Citation. In the Merriam-Webster.com dictionary.
Retrieved, March 6, 2023. from
https://www.merriam-webster.com/dictionary/Chican
a

Can you delay the baby in your belly?
Apa wishes to nap, and his caramel eyes survive
another 18 construction hour job, of installing itchy
insulation.. Ama twenty, first time in a new country,
says she'll try, but she is due today, and she needs his
help filling out the English hospital documentation.
They sit in the pick-up truck.
 In the Emergency side of the parking lot.
The year before, she was playing volleyball with her
friends and going to dances in her village.
She whispers to her younger sister and tells her to go
to bed.
She sneaks out with her soon to be husband, a
nineteen year old runaway hopeful for his love,
doesn't foreshadow his soon to be betrayal, when she
finds out what he promised is not like he said.
Like a hunter shooting an innocent flying dove.

Natural and scruffy mustache snores a tune in gray,
his Carhartt coat blankets his tired pose from a long
day.
He was fourteen when he was told to leave his home
and take the bus up North, call us if you ever feel

alone and make sure to include the wire transfer with
the code.
Now twenty-seven, he smoked a bet for a son, "Una
Mija " doesn't call for the party to light the expensive
cigars.

The father thinks he is getting a boy, celebrates with
the smell of burning hand rolled leaves, the mom
finds out her husband has another child in the way by
the woman who he said was no longer his friend.
He toys with a smirk when he deceives.

The nurses said Mexican women have too many kids,
Ama cries from the contractions and curses them out
as she conceives.

Racist stares need no interpretations!

The little girl gets to know her dad, named; **Sacrifice**
and nickname **"I'm always working."**
So watch a Chicana celebrate with a shot of
tequila"Cazadores" at the bar

Her inner coach tells herself: "Look at me B&t#!"
She sees her pupils through the nightclub, graffiti
wall bathroom mirror.
"You are alive, I see you looking fly"!
AND? AND? AND?
Nobody gives a f*#k about you! (SILENCE)
It's all good, let that S#!t roll off your shoulders.
Hear the music outside waiting for you to get this
party started!

It's time to start giving a f*%k about yourself!

she knows to always bring her own cash, she is told
by her father free drinks is for ho#*.
She dances like her mom did at her age, rejecting
men left and right she feels so good telling them NO!

Her father tells her; she shouldn't fix, lift, or attempt
manly-type things.

Watch a Chicana lose validation, in comparison to
their prodigy son, she will never be to her parents
made to feel like she is enough.
Watch a Chicana's solitude play rock, paper, scissors
with more than two shifts.

She learns how to unload semi trucks, move
furniture, and cashiers during the night, losing her
sleep.

Watch a Chicana's wheels take on more than she
should.

Watch a Chicana be told it means she is small and not
from this part or that part of the country.
A Chicana proud, her Azteca spirit unbound,
Defying the shipping and receiving labels, the boxes
around.
Her heritage of healers stands tall and the sage is
firm.

A warrior of love, no boundaries to divide, when our
parents have been coming from the other side.
Her corridos echoes true, a fierce, powerful sound,
Her "you're doing too much" strength and her "why
do you gotta be so extra?" nurturing beauty, forever
unbound.

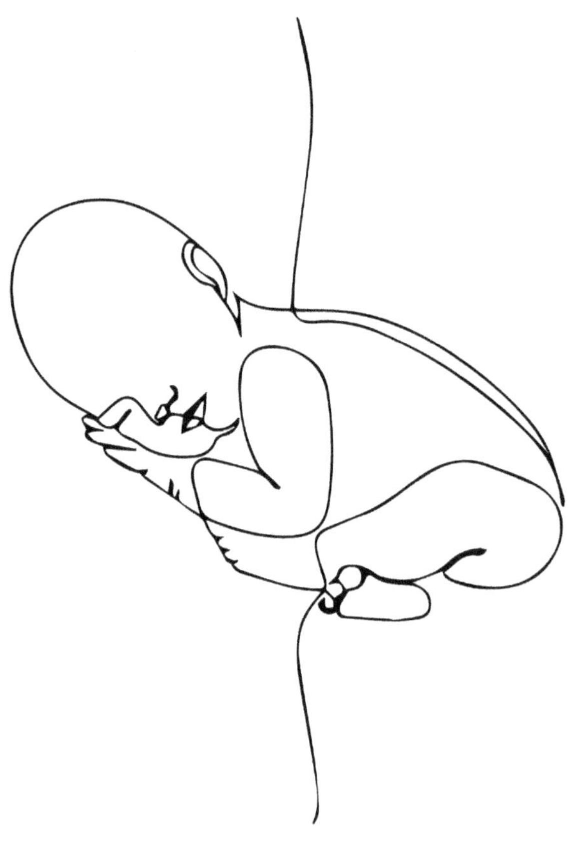

Absence

Fluttering wings fade, first from the tree,
Childhood is not so pretty, when you abandon
the seed.

A monarch butterfly touches my shoulder.
"Hold still, as he snatches the wings.
Boy from this hood says:
"The butterfly he stepped on is now sleeping"
Stillness echoes with whispers,
Love's violin leads a symphony, the orchestra
plays.

Infinite eyes when she turns twenty one sees
love's path, and she can't tell the difference when
intimate aggression is normally the same.
Freckled autumn soul, her silence whimpers, her
chest is knotted.
An act of ugly torches her pain.
Red flags and topaz streams,
Trumpets and drums crescendos.

Love's delicate grace.
Ballroom, an empty space,

Echoes of a woman's voice to a man he says she complains, not a devotion's embrace.

Love's clarinet
Butterfly ghost takes flight,
Fragile, fleeting, innocent, sensible tears blur her sight.
Double cello, a repetitive tune
My father loved my mother this way too.

Cuca

Prickly cactuses cradled my grandma when she was born
and mothered her poor. Handmade tortillas are the
best when they come naturally from the ground corn.
Her stepfather smacks his lips and says he wants a
taste of hers.

Her mother says she is making up stories and angrily
scolds.

She places a note under a rock for her farmer admirer.
He comes by dusk and preps her room by the next
dawn. They get down like that back in the day, says
survival led them to each other, her heart was the
same.

She wears her best dress, he picks white lilies for her,
he vows for her hand and kisses her thanks her for
her love.

Tears nourish the soil, the land she delicately seeds.
She whimpers at her past pain in the rows.
"I think I have a creature," she yells. Her water
bursts, presently irrigating the crops.
Her belly didn't show, how could she know.
Her husband says **"PUSH"** as he tends to the bloody
crown.

Post-Partum Depression, a common misconception to label a SPELL on her head by false friends; village witches who want to see her slurping her food in her bed.

The steaming sun over the green mountain trails boils her woven basket shoes with blisters.

Cuca squints at the river; she wants her youthful reflection back and asks the foaming tides if she can reach for her beauty by sinking down.

The next day,
He ties her to the bark, kisses her forehead his love language to her, before he sparks a fire cooking in the field food from the farm, and promises to not let her drown.

9 to 5

A corporate office man named Jose changed his name to Joe. Truth is his resume was not getting any hits on going corporate.
Now he says his boss praises him for being articulate in his new role.

To go with the flow, so he puts on a show.

The warehouse lead says her boss likes it when she tells the rest not to act up, you know give her a clipboard.

She'll act nose up, like she's all that.

The blue-collar man says he can get any day off if he wants because his boss likes that he does overtime and never requests vacation at all.

His perfect attendance stands tall, his family misses him, they don't have quality time, his relationships fall.

From a performance review after the first 30 days through video call :

CEO: "You are not a Latina Token, but we need you to be our face to them, more like a spokesperson."

"Can you recommend the best taco, enchilada, or margarita spot?"

"You are well-spoken for your race, which is impressive because you don't act like the rest of the Mexicans, you are not like them, you are the exception".

Words of my Momma.

Barefoot child running underneath the sun, her hair
braided, she actions herself, enough of the games.
Be a fighter, she's told, as the oldest of her world was
to shovel love unto others more.
Eagle soaring as her guidance and her youthful
mother friend.
She feels unprotected when her panic scabs her knee.
Is that all you got?
"Dear child, knuckle your fists and toughen up. Life
gets much harder than this."

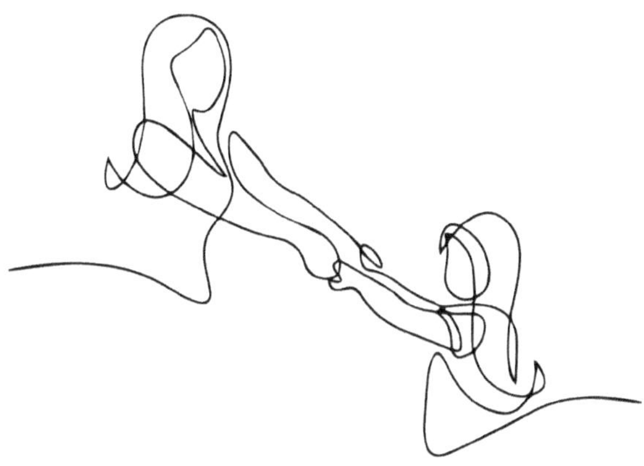

The time I snuck inside an 84 Dorado

In '97, a thrill-seeking notion,
I snuck into an '84 Dorado, a car of my father's
devotion.

Playboy mags and leather steering wheel,
Suede rooftop and the thrill of the steal.

At 5 years old, a curious thought
I pressed my hand over my lips to stay quiet, sparkles
and tassels models galore

I was on a secret mission, zero supervision, I wanted
to explore.

My eyes gleamed with a mischievous riot.
My heart racing with excitement, as I hid from sight.
I yearned for a life of glitz and glam, just like that
car's design,
But with age and wisdom came the knowledge that
true joy lies within the mind.

Lonely Wolf

Amidst the howling of a man so lost,
The wolf within him bore the cost.
The wolf was a lonely boy.
His fierce she-wolf dark shades hide what she
knows
boy sleeping with free cornbread - lady dry
heaving depression in bed
Prison boy wants to escape-
Shrouded secrets from his sight.
The prison boy, with keys in hand,
Locked himself and his love in a barren land.
A weak boy, drowning in alcohol's embrace,
As his lady looked out the window with a
newborn in her arms, shaking the baby
aggressively in frustration.
The unrealistic boy, seeking perfection's light,
Ego-stroked girls for fleeting validation's sight.
A childish boy, tuning life out with damaged
girls,
Licking unhealed wounds in a world of swirls.
But temporary fantasies can't lead a home,
As he tells her it's not romance and leaves her
alone, dancing to the same song.
The insecure boy fails to see,

She's mourning her worth, and who she used to
be.
In the howling of this man so lost,
Sacrificing their time, their purpose soul's true
cost, they had a life of their own, a woman's
defeat is choosing a man and rusting her crown,
losing her values and forgetting her throne.

My first time, where are the fireworks?

When I had my first kiss, I was sitting on a rock mount overlooking a muddy river.

Sitting on the rock mount, like a bird in a nest,
Overlooking the river, where the mud does rest.
Childhood friends, but now so much more,
A crush that grew, a feeling to explore.

I knew him from childhood.
We rode bikes together once.

His spider web tattoo, and his mustache to wear.
Skipping school, to be with him in secret,

I kissed him with my eyes open and felt a knot in my chest.
My first kiss, where are the fireworks and sparks?
Like the movies and shows, with all their arts.
But reality strikes, it's not always a dream,
Sometimes a moment, just isn't what it seems.

He politely moved my hair out of his way, and bit a tint of
blue on my lip aggressively.
My lips felt wet afterward, and I wondered if they had
grown. The moment was a cringy blur.

Childhood friends, but now a first love?

Compliments to a Holy City

Chicago, my dear,
Where the wind whispers tales of hope and fear.
In the red, green, and pink line I am the first act,
A beacon of light for those in lack.
 Will it feed the kids I teach in the south, west and
Little village tonight?
I am the brutal winter, unrelenting and fierce,
But my slush cradles the slow pulse of those in need
of a pierce.
I am the forty oz of liquor, a vice for some,
But a solace for the troubled, their souls on the run.
Even the smell of a rat in my alleyway,
Is a reminder of the struggle and plight that everyday,
Faces the brave souls who call this city their home,
Yet they rise above it, they never roam.
For Chicago, you are more than just a place on a
map,
You are a beating heart, a fire that never loses its
snap.
Compliments to a Holy City, Chicago, my dear,
For your spirit and resilience, we will always cheer.

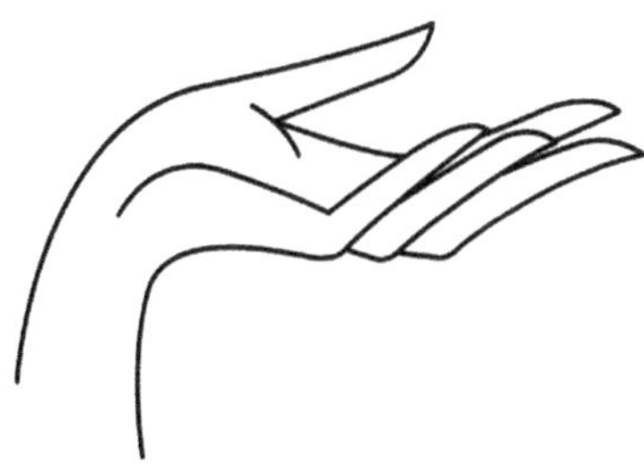

ESL

A boy from my hood
His house smells like sweat and cats
Like he mooned a police car once
And we ran away after that
After his mom, ran the streets for sex work
Left him alone
He cried and jumped up and down, his fists balled up,
I ran inside to find some sweet or spicy snacks, he
wasn't in the mood for any of that.
I could tell he didn't know who his dad was
He called him Superman, we argued, I said it wasn't
true because my dad didn't sound as cool.
He taught me my first English words
A middle finger could mean the same too

Free licks

Both playing a tid for a tad game, jealousy a toxic tale.
"Let me see your phone," he demanded,
And in that moment, love was stranded.

Our love was immature, and young.

Another college friend turned into playful flirting,
theater class, open invitation to his room for rehearsal
not the real intention.

Take a step back, his advances for a kiss, not an ideal
dream for someone I used for a tease.

Being choosy, his attention to drinking, parties, and
nightstands.

Non-committal we both rode the carousel of deceit.
He was, entertaining Twitter, Snapchat, and I.G b***

He accused me of deceit and lies,
Mind was clouded with mistrust,
And our relationship was turning to dust.

I said I would leave for good, and thought our love
wouldn't survive like it should.

Uber nightstand, dirty bra left behind, says his
memory blurs

When I was gone.

Late-night fights and tear-stained sheets,
Our love was now filled with defeats.
But we found the strength to leave it behind, and seek
counsel
For well-being and peace of mind.

A new beginning to start each day.

No longer chained to toxic hold,
Free to embrace a love that's bold.
A love that cherishes and uplifts,
With free licks of joy, laughter, and bliss.

Bills are due

Tomorrow comes, and paper will cut her off.
Deal cards the same way I lost yesterday.
Asks for time to pause to catch up with dues.

Dusk arrives
The body needs to see the crows laugh,
HAHAHAAA, they stole her eyes.
Tied to a stake,
She lets them poke at
her scabs.

Delight

Illustrating lost causes signed away carving your name.
You are my joy.
Even when a profound stroke smells like B.S. from afar
dancing with each other, my chest trembles a beat
Who's the Dj, the Devil or God?

Arrogance runs deep in my blue veins
I grip tight to impracticality
Searching for qualities, I can't find in myself.

we are two in one
Finally, we are strangers
We are none.
The man holds his head held high.
After he feels salty

The way you lift me in the air.
If you are an error? Why am I dismissing your flaws?
Who is the blindest?
The one with no sight
or the one that doesn't want to perceive?

Tough Spine

Injury disc herniation, wear and tear at age 29
Crawling by the Mudd, scraped knees, oh, I'm so
behind getting to this finish line, losing the balance of
priorities, unhealthy spinal sores, aches, inflammation
throbbing, and painful moans
3-6 months feeling so depressed and numb

Naproxen prescribed medication, suicidal ideation;
the lake looks attractive if I taste the waves.
Taking on more and more, until my legs collapsed to
the ground
Recovery without patience is like coming back with
no strength or vengeance.
Agonizing but courageous

Differences

Not present at school.
He was speeding to a secret retreat
At twenty-one, I was seventeen

Spider web, black ink
Trapped me in
Nor did I question him

Foam wave tips
"Sit here."
Fuck it, a beach with no sand
I envision something else.

Feather earrings flew off into the autumn path.
Caressed my hair, politely out of his way

The unorganized boy moved closer.

His criminal moist lips against my virgin ones

This isn't like the movies; his touch isn't soft.

Limited Liability

Stayed up testing my academics all night
Pushing shifts to get good tips I'm talking about this
restaurant life
Mexicans in the back cooking for another man's wife

College-bound, they say, is what moves.
Backpack heavy, heavy-duty fees, my back is sweat
aching when I can't carry these books.
Tired 15-hour days, 4-hour commutes.

Fake smiling ugly faces, wondering how I make good
grades when I have no laptop mac or dorm room and
we are sitting in the same places.

Ah, let's face it: interviews are crazy if your name is
not Karen, Fiona, or Stacey.
Unfortunately, we moved on with another candidate.
We keep your file, so you can place it next time.

Psuedo Mom

Few years of the second-hand store
I styled that shit and called it boutique
What's impossible to a girl that's poor?

Braids and hair so tight, clean and brushed those shoe
and laces hang dry overnight, pressed iron crease a
line on the jeans so right, who would know
What my real life hides?

As the oldest child, I had to protect the rest
cook, bathe them, and pick up the mess
Fuck negativity, pretend like they had extracurricular
activity, played like we belong to the bougie life.
I had a dollar store craft, a bike, and too much pride
to accept a ride.

Playing Psuedo Mom made me want to sue my mom.
I realized all she does is grind even though she is
trapped in the trauma of her own mind.
Her trauma is no longer mine.

The Subdivision dream

Flew to Mexico to get to know me
Breathe the land, mango, authentic tortillas, no
Milagros, and taco meats to your taste.
Eat so fresh and well, ancestor's laughter wealth

Came back home enclosed, feeling jailed
Not so neighborly neighborhood feeling out of my shell
Can't afford cookie-cutter subdivision
Mortgage too much over the belt

Money for Camping

4th-grade field trip
A hood girl never has been camping
I want to go!
I had never had a sleeping bag before.

Selling for months Twizzlers, M&M's, Hershey's,
and classic chocolate bars.
Stopping at the projects, apartments, and regular cat
lady homes, going door to door.

"How come you are dressed like the Avon or Mary
Kay lady? said the neighborhood kid.

Dropped off at the Mexican supermarket, a lady
hustling, people asking her to quit.

My boxes of candy almost sold out
sirens can be seen as the police are en route
Women behind suspiciously head out

Minding my business
The officer snatches my box, "Are you selling this
sh**?"
Shocked at his words, never been camping or heard a
police cuss

"Are you selling your body?"
"I am only 11," I said nervously, feeling embarrassed.
I answered back
I hadn't done anything wrong.

"Show me your I.D."
Quickly grabbed my library card.
"No, that isn't enough."

No phone at the time, tears and finger-pointing
The cop drove away, and no box or money returned;
it felt like a sting.

Vending Machine

The two little girls step away from the party.
Leaving their moms in the venue, away from the
lobby
"I want a chocolate bar," says one, "chips for
me," says the other
as they skip in the hallway waving their dollars.

Heading for the vending machine while the two
moms enjoy the music
Without a clue, when a man chases them to trap
them in his room
If only they knew how with his eyes, he
undressed them
salivating with his predatory intention.

Holding hands tight, one says, "do you know
where to go"?
"I know the way. Whatever you do, don't let go."
of the girls losing direction, clenched with panic.
"We can't run slow."

The man is catching up to them, smirking and
laughing

"STOP right there, you nasty son of a B!+**,"
said another man. At the same time, his arms
suffocated the weirdo with a chokehold.

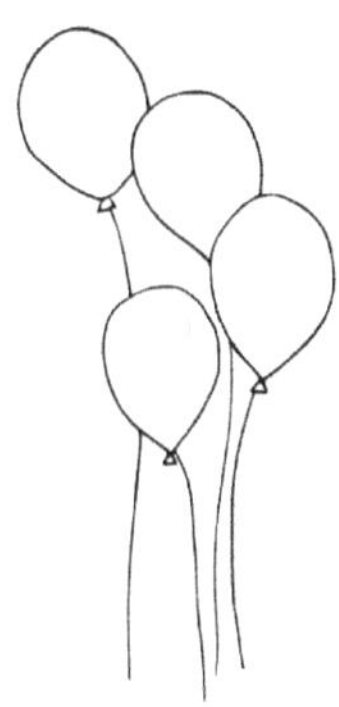

If I should

Shoulda, woulda, coulda don't exist
Don't listen to the voices of pessimists.

I am madly in hate with unpaid loans, loaning
my time, and sourly sitting at the job.
Jobless passions, what is a poet doing behind a
cubicle?

Sincerely
I should